ISBN-13: 978-0692364864
ISBN-10: 0692364862

Dedicated to my pastor, Pastor Mercy Jones,

who taught me how to both live and die for Christ's sake.

IT'S TIME TO DIE

"I Brought You Here to Die"

Several years ago I had a conversation with the Lord about life and destiny, and what He spoke to my spirit that day changed my walk with Him forever. I was at a place in my life where my hunger for God was deepening by the day, and all I wanted to do was get closer to Him. I had recently rededicated my life to the Lord, and was planted in a ministry that was challenging me to grow spiritually. Our church was in the midst of a corporate fast, and it was a wonderful season of personal development for me. I felt so alive—which is why the Lord's Words to me seemed so surprising.

He said, *"I brought you here to die."* Needless to

say, these words were not what I expected to hear. What He showed me next, however, cleared up any confusion I may have had and opened my eyes to a most profound revelation about life in Christ.

The Mountain

Immediately following those words, the Lord placed an image in my mind's eye. All of a sudden I saw myself standing at the base of a large mountain looking upward. I glanced at the peak of the mountain, and somehow knew that I had to eventually reach that point. As I stood there gazing at the vast expanse

of this great mountain,
the Lord began to speak
to me about the perilous
journey ahead.

First, He reminded me
about the types of things
that occur in the human
body when it is exposed
to extreme elevations.
Our body is not equipped
to function, let alone exist
indefinitely at extremely
high altitudes. The higher
the altitude is, the more

deadly the conditions become. For instance, the temperature plummets as you move from the base of a mountain to its peak. If care is not taken, you could easily freeze to death from hypothermia or suffer from frostbite. In severe cases of frostbite, the flesh can become so frozen that it is no longer functional and must be amputated.

Morbid I know. But this is just one of many ailments the flesh will experience on the way up a mountain. In addition to freezing temperatures, there is also the threat of hypoxia, or lack of oxygen. There is less air pressure at higher elevations, which means there is less air available for breathing. Less air means less oxygen—the very molecule utilized in blood circulation, heart and lung regulation, and brain activity. Without oxygen, your brain cells begin to die rapidly, and fluid begins to build up around the lungs. Breathing becomes more and more difficult until you become weak, immobilized and eventually die. So as I stand in front of this mountain I realize that to climb it will undoubtedly cost me my life. Yet everything inside of me knows that this is exactly what I am supposed to do.

But why? Why in the world would God lead me on a death mission when He is the giver of life?

The revelation hit my spirit instantly: There are places that God wants to take me that my flesh cannot go. There are heights in the realm of the spirit that cannot sustain flesh. To reach my full potential in God, I must allow my flesh to die.

The death of my flesh empowers my spirit. God is a Spirit, and He desires that we worship and fellowship with Him from a place in our spirit and a place of truth (John 4:24). That place within the realm of the spirit is a high and holy place, where Truth Himself dwells:

> *"For thus saith the high and lofty One that inhabiteth eternity, whose name is Holy; I dwell in the high and holy place, with him also that is of a contrite and humble spirit, to revive the spirit of the humble, and to revive the heart of the contrite ones."* (Isaiah 57:15 KJV)

To reach this high and holy place where His presence dwells, we must leave the low realms of the flesh and travel to the realm of the spirit. The mountain represents the journey from flesh to spirit—a journey that we as believers must make. It is a humbling and harrowing journey no doubt, and your flesh will suffer on the way up. But at the end of the journey, when the price is paid, every humble and a contrite heart finds themselves in the presence of the Master Himself, who revives and strengthens their spirit with His own Hand.

The base of the mountain symbolizes the place where our spiritual journey begins. It is here we experience salvation and become empowered by the Spirit of God to go higher in Him. It is from this place that we start the trek upwards, continually shedding the "old man" and being transformed more and more into the image of Christ. Unfortunately, many believers never leave the base of the mountain. Out of fear, complacency, or ignorance of their need to climb higher in the Spirit, they park their spirits right at the moment of salvation. The problem with living life from this place is that the flesh remains intact and the spirit remains weak, as it is not positioned for empowerment.

You don't want to camp out at the base of the mountain, never growing beyond your salvation experience. We should always maintain a

Philippians 3:13-14 mentality when it comes to our spirituality:

> *"Brethren, I count not myself to have apprehended: but this one thing I do, forgetting those things which are behind, and reaching forth unto those things which are before, I press toward the mark for the prize of the high calling of God in Christ Jesus."*

What is the high calling? The fulfilment of

your purpose and destiny in Christ! The mark we press towards? The glory of God! The glory of God is His tangible, manifested presence, the fullness of His glory in every area of your life. His presence is the prize! The peak of the mountain represents the place where the fullness of His presence dwells.

Every act of obedience to God is a step up the mountain, and every step draws you closer to God's glory. As you move up the mountain, your flesh is getting weaker, and your spirit is growing stronger. The stronger your spirit, the greater your capacity to receive God's glory into your life—and the more glory you receive, the easier and more beautiful your entire existence becomes.

This is why spiritual stagnation is your enemy,

because the weights of this world and the downward pull of your flesh towards the earth will keep you from gaining ground in the spirit. The same way that the death of the flesh empowers the spirit, spiritual inactivity empowers the flesh and allows it to thrive. The journey up the mountain is a spiritual activity that causes the natural, fleshly weights to fall off so that you become more "fit" and more effective spiritually.

Do not fear the journey ahead, because the Holy Spirit of God is with you every step of the way. He will lead you to a glorious end every time! The benefits of salvation do not end once your spirit is reborn. That is simply the beginning of life in Christ. The Bible says in 2 Corinthians 3:18 and Romans1:17 that we are to go from glory to glory and from faith to faith and that the "path of the righteous grows brighter and brighter with the passing of the day." (Proverbs 4:18).

We each have a work to do for the Lord and a godly purpose to fulfil. Our spirit must be empowered in order to accomplish this work. Continue to climb until you reach the place where your spirit has conquered and overcome your flesh. Never settle for less than the fullness of God!

We see in Exodus 19:20-33 and Exodus 34:29-35 how Moses pressed into greater realms of glory and became empowered for the great task ahead of him. God often called to him from the mountain and Moses always answered the call and went up to commune with Him. As a result, the glory of God transfigured his flesh and caused Moses' face to shine like the sun!

"When Moses came down from Mount Sinai with the two tablets of the covenant law in his hands, he was not aware that his face was

radiant because he had spoken with the LORD."
(Exodus 34:29)

Moses' mountaintop experience is a picture of what life in Christ looks like for those believers who are willing to "make the climb". God is calling to each of us from a high place, and He desires that we come up to commune with him on a deeper level. Each of us has our own "mountain of God" to climb. You may have already climbed to a certain point in your spiritual journey and feel content with where you are, but there is so much more glory to be revealed. Keep on climbing!

The Call to Die

We are all called to die—to die to our flesh. Spiritually speaking, the word "flesh" denotes more than just one's physical body. The flesh is the human nature without God, or man's "lower" nature. It is often used to identify the unregenerate, sensual side of man that is not in subjection to God. You see, we are man on three levels: spirit, soul, and body. We were created in the image of God as a spirit, given a soul (our mind, will, and emotions), and housed in a body (see Genesis 1:27-28, 2:7). Created in the image of God, our spirit has been given dominion over all things in the earth—including our own body and soul. It is the from the body and soul

that fleshly desires arise—
which is why they must
remain in subjection to
your born-again spirit.

The fleshly side of man
gravitates towards
fulfilling carnal desires and
lusts, and has an affinity
for the things of this
world. Fleshly desires are
often diametrically
opposed to the desires of
your regenerated (born-
again) spirit—one is

always working against the other. To fulfill the desires of one, the other must be denied. Jesus said this about denying yourself:

> "Then Jesus said to His disciples, "If anyone wishes to come after Me, he must deny himself, and take up his cross and follow Me. "For whoever wishes to save his life will lose it; but whoever loses his life for My sake will find it." (Matthew 16:24.-25 NIV)

And again in John 12:25 He said:

> _"Anyone who loves their life will lose it, while anyone who hates their life in this world will keep it for eternal life."

The command to die to the lower nature is not just noble, it is necessary. According to Luke 14:27, we cannot even be a follower of Christ if we refuse to "take up our cross" and die to the flesh:

"And whoever does not carry their cross and follow me cannot be my disciple."

Jesus was adamant about dying to one's own flesh because He understood the fierce and unique battle between the flesh and the spirit. Unbelievers do not have this same struggle because their spirit is not alive unto God. The voice of the flesh reigns supreme in their lives.

But as Christians, our spirit has been "made alive" by being connected to God, the Source of life:

> *"And you hath he quickened, who were dead in trespasses and sins; Wherein in time past ye walked according to the course of this world, according to the prince of the power of the air, the spirit that now worketh in the children of disobedience: Among whom also we all had our*

*conversation in times past
in the lusts of our flesh,
fulfilling the desires of the
flesh and of the mind; and
were by nature the children
of wrath, even as others.
But God, who is rich in
mercy, for his great love
wherewith he loved us,
Even when we were dead
in sins, hath quickened us
together with Christ, (by
grace ye are saved;) And
hath raised us up together,
and made us sit together in
heavenly places in Christ*

Jesus..." (Ephesians 2:1-6 KJV)

Therefore, as Paul describes in Romans 7, we have two laws working in our members—the law of the flesh (the unregenerate nature), and the law of the Spirit (the divine nature):

> *"So I find this law at work: Although I want to do good, evil is right there with me. For in my inner being I delight in God's law;*

but I see another law at work in me, waging war against the law of my mind and making me a prisoner of the law of sin at work within me. What a wretched man I am! Who will rescue me from this body that is subject to death? Thanks be to God, who delivers me through Jesus Christ our Lord!" (Romans 7:21-25 NIV)

As Christians, we <u>must</u> crucify the flesh and its deeds because they are in opposition to God and everything He stands for. The flesh is at enmity with the spirit, making it impossible to serve both at once. Since you can't serve two masters, one must die. Christ did that which we could not do for ourselves by freeing us from the power of the sin nature that dwells within us. He crucified His body and took on our sin so that we could experience the life of God. Now we must do what He cannot do for us and make the quality decision to crucify our own flesh, nailing our "old man" to His cross and walking in the newness of life He afforded us through the sacrificing of His own flesh. It is an exercise of our will every time we choose to walk in the Spirit and not fulfill the lusts of the flesh (Galatians 5:16).

"And they that are Christ's have crucified the flesh with the affections and lusts." (Galatians 5:24)

Every time you decide to crucify the flesh and follow after the Spirit of God, you empower your own spirit to have victory in Christ. Paul declared his own "death-to-self" experience in Galatians 2:20:

"I have been crucified with Christ and I no longer live, but Christ lives in me. The life I now live in the body, I live by faith in the Son of God, who loved me and gave himself for me."

Jesus never intended for us to live a flesh-ruled, senses-driven existence. He wanted us to be led by the Spirit of God in all that we do. When flesh is alive and well, it is more difficult to hear the Spirit of God. Kathryn Kuhlman, a minister of the Gospel who had many signs, wonders, and healings follow her ministry, made a powerful statement before an auditorium full of people one day:

> *"Before I came out here tonight, I died a thousand deaths. Kathryn Kuhlman died a thousand deaths before I could even come out here tonight to tell you about Jesus. I died a*

thousand deaths, so that you would not hear the words of Kathryn Kuhlman, but rather hear the words of God."

The Lord knew that in order for us to be empowered for service, the flesh must be crucified. So He, being our great example, made the ultimate sacrifice of His flesh to provide the ultimate service to humanity—salvation for all mankind.

Start Planning Your Funeral!

It's a great day to die! And the sooner the better. Why? Because a greater glory awaits you! When we lay down our fleshly desires, ideals and lifestyles to embrace the way of the Spirit, the presence of God manifests in our lives in a powerful way! As 1 Corinthians 1:29 says, no flesh shall glory in the presence of God, which is exactly why it has to die. Let nothing hinder you from experiencing the fullness of God. Dying to the flesh enables us to be where God is and to do the works that God has called us to do. As long as it is alive, it will fight against that which the Lord wants to accomplish in your life. God wants to see us free from the snares that a life in the flesh entraps us with—substance abuse, sexual addictions and perversion, overeating, gossip, pride, etc. All such vices are born in the flesh. Freedom from flesh comes from liberating your spirit. In the continuation of this book entitled, *"7 Ways to Die"*, I discuss the seven strategies found in the Word of God for attacking the flesh and setting your spirit free.

> *"For whoever wills to save his life will lose it and whoever will lose his life for me will find it." (Matt 16:25 KJV)*

Crucifying the flesh is a choice. New life has been given to us through Jesus Christ but we must choose to walk in it. Renew your mind to the benefits of a life after the "death" of your flesh: productivity, fruitfulness, peace, and freedom from a lifestyle of sin:

> "Verily, verily, I say unto you, Except a corn of wheat fall into the ground and die, it abideth alone: but if it die, it bringeth forth much fruit. He that loveth his life shall lose it; and he that hateth his life in this world shall keep it unto life eternal. If any man serve me, let him follow me; and where I am, there shall also my servant be: if any man serve me, him will my

Father honor." (John 12:24-26 KJV)

God's highest and best life is experienced when we walk in the spirit and mortify the deeds of the flesh. So if you are ready to soar to the heights of life in Christ, just ask yourself the all-important question: are you ready to die?

Prayer of Ascension:

Heavenly Father, I have acknowledged Jesus Christ as my Lord and Savior and I want to go higher in You! I am ready to deny my flesh and empower my spirit with more of Your presence. Let Your Holy Spirit lead to where You are. Show me how to crucify my flesh on a daily basis and walk in the way of the Spirit. Your

Word says that You dwell with the humble and contrite of heart, so I humble myself before You and surrender my life to You. Thank You for reviving my spirit, soul, and body! In Jesus' name, Amen!